My Last Thoughts
about Iraq

To David Winn

My pleasure

Paul Bratton

6/08/2010

My Last Thoughts about Iraq

Paul Batou

To order additional copies of this book, contact:
Xlibris Corporation
1-888-795-4274
www.Xlibris.com
Orders@Xlibris.com
35505

Contents

Poems

This book is for the world to read.

Acknowledgments

1. My mother, who worked hard her entire life to bring my family together. She supported me and helped me succeed in all aspects of my life.
2. My father, with whom I may have had my arguments with but still helped me more than I could understand at the time. I questioned his advice, but I now understand he was making the best decisions possible.
3. My brothers and sisters who withdrew from their schools in order to work and support the family. No matter what, they always spared money so I could buy books and art supplies.
4. My aunt, who, although disabled, still worked hard to finance my studies. Without her, I would not have my degree in pharmacy.
5. My wife, who suffered when I departed for war. Her prayers and support gave me the strength to continue.
6. My friend and relative, Suad Qasha, who translated a majority of my poems and worked very hard to make this book a reality.
7. My nephew, Steven Zaflow, who translated, arranged, and edited these poems. He was a great help to me.
8. My nieces, Zina and Ranna Zaflow, who shared their ideas when I was editing the poems. I can't express my appreciation.
9. To the Iraqi people, especially my relatives and the people of my village, who inspired my thinking through their stories of suffering and their never-ending struggle.
10. To all the American soldiers who went to Iraq for the noble cause to free people under oppression.
11. To my son Augen who helped build my Web site, gave me advice in arranging the poems and editing the pages.
12. To all the Americans who were very generous in their support of my art and poetry. Their love and passion gave me the freedom and strength to achieve the highest goals in my life.

A Note to the Reader

This collection of art and poetry is about my journey as a Mesopotamian. In order to better convey myself, I have written an introduction that will describe my life, ideas, friends, dreams, and thoughts. Please read the introduction, the summary of Iraqi history, and the cleansing of Iraqi Christians from Iraq.

From the Translator

I have come to know Paul since the seventies. We were a bunch of poor young university students with different talents and different ideologies, yet we respected and cared about each other. We were happy to be together, discussing a new novel, walking on the riverside, going to cinemas, attending theatres and concerts. The voices and the smells of those memories are still alive in my head. We were just like a joyful song not yet finished.

Then the first war started, and we were scattered here and there. Doubts, despair, fear, and the unknown started to grow inside us; the long war was able to kill all our dreams and our expectations. Black banners started to rise at street corners or at front doors, each telling the story of a fallen young soldier.

Too many changes happened suddenly and painfully. We lost each other in the chaos of the war; our hearts were frozen, our smiles were sad and dead . . . We were heading toward the hopeless land; we lost the voice of life.

The war ended after eight long years, but we started another war and then came the twelve hard years of economical sanctions. My life was too burdened for me to stay. I left my dear city of Baghdad. Most of us left and were able to start a new journey of life, thanks to these generous democratic countries that opened their doors widely to us; but our Baghdad is still drinking the death of its people, no matter what their identity is. It is a deep, wide painful wound.

I found Paul's Web site after years of disconnecting; I saw his paintings and read his fifteen poems. It was as if I was entering a holy place; I am able to hear the echo of our simple joy that was stolen in a barbaric way. Here in North America, I was able to regain my feelings as a human being; there, we had lost everything. Paul's poems are so realistic, simply because they are able to express the way we used to be and feel inside that republic of fear—Iraq.

What I like in Paul's poems is his ability to draw this completely different, wide picture of life in this old historical city of Baghdad. He focused on the pain, the fear, and the darkness that took over; yet he made a room for confession, forgiveness, and hope. His message through his paintings and his poems is a cry against humiliation of the human dignity, wherever it is; it is a cry for justice and peace.

Paul, you are an inspiration, and I do believe in you . . . Thank you.

Your friend,
Suad Qasha

The Cleansing of the Iraqi Christians

The oppression of Mesopotamia started when the Arabs occupied the land in the seventh century. They used a different method to wipe Christianity from their homeland. Many Christians helped the Muslims fight against Persia in the battle of Quadesia. in which the Arabs defeated the Persian Empire. They expected that the new invaders would give freedom to Christians because Christianity is recognized in their holy book: the Qur'an.

Instead, they imposed a new rule against Christians: either follow their banner and convert to Islam or pay heavy taxes, which many Christians could not afford.

In recent history, the major massacres of the Mesopotamian people occurred in 1828 at Nineveh, in northern Iraq.

In 1843 it was the Bader-Khan massacres; and in 1895 it was the Assyrian and Armenian massacres in Turkey. During the First World War, genocide occurred against the Christians and almost one million people were wiped out.

In 1933, the massacre of Semel forced many Christian villagers to leave their land. My village shared a similar fate in 1961 when strangers ravaged our land. Those strangers were mainly the Kurds, and that territory is now known as Kurdistan in northern Iraq.

Now, the Iraqi Christians have been scattered to many areas around the world. Their villages and cities were conquered, and their history was stolen and placed in museums across the globe.

The American invasion of Iraq made immigration nearly impossible. The majority of Iraqi Christians were leaving their homeland (the homeland that they had lived in since the very beginning of recorded history). These people had fled to places such as Syria, Jordan, and all parts of Europe asking for temporary asylum. Those who remain in Iraq are moving to the northern cities. During the recent invasion, many ancient Sumerian cities in the south were wiped out. The artifacts from those cities were stolen by Iraqi people and sold for next to nothing-not always out of greed but out the desire to survive. The thieves of these artifacts have no connection to the ancient cities. Simply put, it was not their history.

History of Mesopotamia

The Sumerian Civilization 3000-2350 BC

The Akkadian Empire 2350-2112 BC

The Empire of Ur III 2112-2004 BC

Old Babylonian Empire 2004-1600 BC

The Assyrian Empire 1600-626 BC

The Chaldean Empire of Babylon 626-539 BC

Destruction of the Mesopotamian Civilization*

Mesopotamia under the Persians and Greeks 539 BC-AD 637

Mesopotamia Became Iraq under the Arabs AD 637-1258

Iraq under Mongols AD 1258-1432

Iraq under Turkmen Tribes AD 1375-1508

Iraq under the Safavids of Iran AD 1508-1534

Iraq under Ottoman Empire AD 1534-1918

Iraq under British Control AD 1918-1932

The Independence AD 1932

British Intervention AD 1939-1945

Revolution and First Republic AD 1958

The Coup of 1968: Ba'ath and Saddam Rise to Power

War against the Kurdish Region 1973

War with Iran AD 1980-1988

---

* During these periods, the native people of Mesopotamia, now the Christian minority of Iraq, had drastically declined in population and cultural influence. They found themselves in a diaspora as refugees in other countries worldwide while their culture, history, and artifacts were stolen and placed in major museums around the world.

Invasion of Kuwait and The Gulf War AD 1990

Brutal Sanction against Civilians of Iraq AD 1990-2003

American Occupation Known as Operation "Iraqi Freedom" AD 2003

Introduction

Burning of my village and life in Baghdad

There is a question that lingers like a shadow. It is about Mesopotamia, the great civilization that was built on the lands that forged the legend of Gilgamesh. It is about Iraq, a shattered reality from a glorious past. I ask myself, are we the same Assyrians and Chaldeans that gave birth to humanity and culture? There are times when I doubt if we are.

My Last Thoughts about Iraq is the story of my journey since childhood. My story starts with the sound of gunfire and horses in 1961. It starts in a tiny village near the border of Turkey.

It was that day when the savages and Kurds invaded Tin, where God was watching over my aunt, father, mother, brothers, and neighbors as we ran to hide. My parents upheld a very pure Christian philosophy on life. Our savage neighbors were given land to work and farm, but they chose to invade and burn. They broke our walls and ruined the beauty of my home. Tin would no longer be able to hold our secrets and dreams. After a long journey and passing through different cities, we found a new home among new people who spoke Arabic. Baghdad, with its small rooms and narrow allies, was like a city with no lovers. In the capital, we were given borders and assigned new birthdays.

Baghdad was already broken by wars, revolutions, and poverty. It was not a capital for dreamers. We were a family of nine forced to live a new style of life: survival. Under the poverty line, we worked for food; and very few worked for an education. I witnessed many people fail and continue to work to no end.

When I looked back at our first home in Baghdad, I remembered the surrounding city walls, streets, windows, and *shanashil.* I cannot imagine how we were able to live in one house shared by six other families. It was no different from a prison; six rooms, one bathroom, and a small kitchen shared by forty living humans. In the midst of Baghdad, we prayed to God when we were poor, we prayed when we were hungry, and we even prayed for forgiveness when we received bullets.

Behind Baghdad, the memories of different cities existed. The beauty of Kremat and its shanashil. Behind these colored windows, there was always a hidden beauty looking with open eyes at me. My heart was young and fresh, like an orange from Balad. I could only look at women; they were like palm trees from Basrah. I kept looking and walking, praying to God before bedtime for sensual dreams.

I had a dream that I caught the northern air and the southern scents. It was a dream of a noisy city waking at dawn from prayers of God's greatness. I dreamed of Victory Plaza, a victory that we never had. There was a statue of Jawad dedicated to freedom, a freedom that we never had. It was a dream of a body floating on the ocean, calling for Iraq.

It is my memories that cradle me. They walk with me miles at a time, down narrow streets, through crowded markets, hearing the gentle voices at the café in passing. Oh, my dear Ishtar! I don't remember how many times I've loved! I don't remember if I've forgotten a thousand kisses, or if I've escaped from a thousand hugs.

A sin hides in my shadows. Maybe it's more than one. I am prepared to confess every failing of mine to God. Even if I am prepared to atone, how will the many sins of Iraq be cleansed?

My last thoughts reflected my memories in downtown bars, prostitutes, the many homeless, and the suffering poor. The broken hearts all spoke the language of Iraq, they all carried the sins of Iraq. They all became drunk and deluded with no alcohol.

I still had moments of pleasure in Baghdad. I had friends who surrounded me with love, who surrounded me with passion. We spoke with one another; we played; we partied; we danced and forgot all of our troubles. We walked along Al-Saddon Street, a famous street in downtown Baghdad. We would walk down the Tigris and Abu Nuwas street. We enjoyed movies; we made jokes and lived a carefree life. No matter how bad anything became, we always felt stronger with each other. Without mentioning names, I would say that my friends and I were strongly bound to one another.

I recall how we would dance, or how I would hug my lover in slow motion while listening to various Assyrian singers. Those moments in Iraq were different from any other moments in my life. I could close my eyes and find myself gliding back into these memories. I find myself freed by the music, and I find I am able to reach across the darkened sky and touch the stars. In Iraq, we still have friends. In Baghdad, we still have lovers. In Mesopotamia, there are still singers, writers, and artists. There are still those who will mention our names, those who will record our stories, those who will satisfy our hunger, those who will bring us joy; there are still those who will deliver us to a new life.

The many artists, countless writers, and abundant singers hold the keys to our prison doors. Through their path, real freedom will be delivered—not through oppression and war.

After I finished my elementary years in Catholic school, I transferred to a junior high public school. It was a drama that taught me that I had enemies. Education was pushed aside. Our new lesson plans taught us that the British, Americans, Europeans, Israelis, and the West were evil infidels. We learned that we were truly an oppressed group of people. Fighting replaced education; guns replaced books; war shadowed peace; and innocence was stolen, time after time. In all Arab countries, they have pencils, paper, and a butcher knife. In all Arab countries, there are statues dedicated to victory.

Knowing the truth behind all of this is a drama that unfolds before your very eyes. This drama holds the truth behind our falling and destruction.

My love, Ishtar, you are the beauty of Babylon in a world that does not understand the history and the secrets of love. I am responsible for what will happen to me, no one else.

My Last Thoughts about Iraq is my cry to heaven. Why did you forsake Babylon? The mistakes made occurred more than three thousand years ago.

I cannot atone for them. I cannot gain your forgiveness. I cannot wash away the sins that burden my people.

Connection to Gypsies

My Last Thoughts about Iraq is about my connection to gypsies. Gypsies who had no homes, identity, or land. Gypsies who share similar dances, songs, and stories. I played the guitar like a gypsy; every stroke of my finger is a release of anger and passion. Later came singing, painting, dancing and waiting. Waiting for my path to escape.

The Gypsy style fills my life with joy and mystery, as well as romance and complete freedom to express my self through poetry and painting. I will listen to their singing for days and days, with passion, while my eyes are closed. Through them, I discovered Goya, Lorca, and Picasso. I discovered Spain, which became a dream destination to live in.

While I experienced the horror of death, war, hunger, and sorrow, I looked back to Mesopotamia and Uruk. Babylon was an experience of love and life. Ishtar and the gods of Sumer once awarded power and beauty to the lands.

It was my desire to escape with a gypsy to freedom. A freedom not rewarded by war and oppression, but through a wish. The same wish that a bird would make when it migrates to a peaceful land. Freedom became a desire for water and bread to share with the poor and homeless. Freedom was having a pencil to write, a crayon to color, and a guitar to play.

Freedom was the voice of the soldiers in a battlefield to muffle the sounds of bullets. It was my desire to stand under the rain and wash my sins, sadness, and memories spent away in a prison called Iraq. Freedom was having my anger toward all nations who sanctioned the dreams of the Iraqi children. Those nations stole our smiles, medicine, and food from the hands of the many women, children, and elderly. Freedom became my anger and my cry to God, who would order praying and fasting, as well as rewarding virgins to killers. Freedom was my escape from a country that had kidnapped my rights and allowed the killing of the innocent.

War with Iran

My eyes were open as I watched the destruction and horror between Iran and Iraq as they fought for land that concealed the filth that governed all nations: oil. While serving in the medical unit on the front line, I learned how to collect body parts. I watched as the human body was ravaged. Each side called their dead martyrs; each death would be rewarded in heaven. Some even carried a key to paradise while their families ate rocks and swallowed their sadness so they could pray to God and praise their leaders.

There was one story that I would never forget during the war. It was dark outside; our light came from tiny stars shining far away. We had a case of a young soldier complaining of chest pains. After the doctor gave him a complete exam, he concluded that the soldier had a heart attack or angina. The doctor asked me for nitroglycerin tablets to control his pain or any medication for arteriovascular disease, if available. I told him that in the front line, we treated only wounded soldiers. I could only offer aspirin for this soldier. He should have never been here on the front lines; he needed a transfer to the nearest city hospital. Unfortunately, we were in Kurdish territory; and all the roads were closed due to curfew.

We were all worried about the young soldier as we stood above his bed discussing alternatives for help. He looked at us with a smile and said, "My friends, go sleep! Don't worry about me. And if I die, throw me out to the wild animals." He passed away the next morning on his journey to the hospital. Many soldiers felt happy when their wounds were minor or when they became disabled. Many of them shot their toes in order to be dismissed from the army. Some even looked forward to death.

We have blamed one person for the suffering and destruction of Iraq. If Saddam Hussein is really to blame for all that we have contributed to him, then he is a very intelligent and strong person.

With no education, he rose up from a street gang to become the leader of Iraq. As a dictator, he controlled the future of millions of Iraqis.

He controlled the army, the educators, the musicians, the artists, the professionals, the reporters, and even the tribes in Iraq. Some might say that he accomplished all of this with his secret squad of police; but I believe that we are the only ones to blame. He was only one man, and we gave him the tools to oppress.

We had given him the tools to control our lives; we had given him our freedom. We surrendered to his ambition when we fought in his army. The fact is that we never really had freedom before his rule. For centuries, we had been trained to follow the orders of so many invaders; we had never been allowed to think for ourselves or to seek an education.

As an example, take a typical Iraqi family. The father is the one in charge, and the wife has no rights and cannot object to any of the man's decisions. The rest of the women in the family are prohibited from seeking an education, working, leaving the house unveiled, or even falling in love. Everyone living under the man's roof is obliged to follow his order, no questions asked.

I used to hear a lot in the streets or at cafés. People would say, "This is God's wish." Or "This is our destiny." I've heard people mutter, "God will give, and God will take." And "Pray to God and ask for forgiveness." "The poor will have heaven." "Jihad in the name of God will be rewarded."

We were raised to obey the mullah, or for Christians, obey the priest; to love your leader, and respect your superiors. When you believe in sacrifice, you will give anything. We were surrounded by images of our leaders. Whether it was at home or at work, we were surrounded by images of Saddam. It was our decision to live that way. I will never say that Saddam is the only one responsible for my misery.

Sanction

Good morning, Iraq. Good morning to the poor, the hopeless, the powerless. Good morning, my friends. You all remember when the dawn would glow in Baghdad. It was a peaceful time with the sound of Fairuz, the Lebanese singer. It was so relaxing to hear her voice every morning. Her voice overcame the sound of machinery in our busy streets. She gave our life a different taste and gave us the courage to be happy. To support each other was one way to survive the ugly regime. We had turned all the real stories into jokes, and the sad ones to prayers. We behaved as if we were happy. Every Iraqi has a long story and much to talk about. We create a reason for every event. We create a positive conclusion behind sad events. As people used to say, "You may hate something, but it might turn out to be for your benefit." In other words, accept whatever happens to you because it is your destiny.

Nighttime in Baghdad was dark, with moonlight dancing over the Tigris River. A breeze would pass, surrounding us with aspirations to dream. All nations kill Iraqis. They did so not by wars or invasions only. A majority of those murders are by malnutrition, disease, lack of medicine, and lack of general care. All nations sanction Iraqi civilians. Simple things such as vaccines, aspirin, asthma inhalers, antibiotics, vitamins, clean water, and bread will save many; yet all these were sanctioned by the United Nations.

They punish millions of civilians because of one person: Saddam. No one seems to care that the powerless Iraqis are the ones suffering, not him. Now, Iraqis torture each other just to survive. Every day is a struggle. Ethnic struggle, revenge, and jihad have won in Iraq. There is no longer a place for fine art and music. There is no place for these things in a land that gave us the *Epic of Gilgamesh*.

In America

My Last Thoughts about Iraq is a journey with Ishtar from Sumer and Uruk to the other side of the ocean. In that paradise, I can wash away my sadness. It was once a wish to reach the land of fog, blue eyes, and blonde hair. It was in this Christian land that I could recover my dreams. I saw Ishtar and Gilgamesh and the gates of Babylon all gathered in a large hall. I cried to Ishtar, "They took everything beautiful from my land and left my wounded body for the vultures!"

Oh Ishtar, they asked me if I was from Iraq. Did I look different? Ishtar, shall I hide my identity, my face, and my smile? Ishtar, as long as I am from Iraq, there are always thieves and strangers close to me. How am I to escape? Ishtar, I am an American now; but my heart was born in Iraq.

In America, I focused my eyes on a morning in New York. The sky was blue and the sea was quiet. It was a beautiful city embracing beautiful people. There came dust and destruction, as well as death. The horror took my memory far back to Iraq; I looked into my mother's eyes and asked her if she saw what the terrorists did to our civilization. She replied, "Son, they've chased us to our new home."

In a dream on April 9, 2003, the statue of Saddam came crashing down. The dictator is gone, and the land is free. The Iraqis are free. Will I return to walk down the same roads as my father? Will I walk the same streets I did as a child? Will the cities be the same? Where are my friends, relatives, and the world that has thrived in my memories?

Restore my history, bring back Ishtar and Enlil; teach the world of their tale. Bring back the birds, the orange and palm trees, the many homes with their families inside. Open the museums, the playgrounds, great theatres, even the bars so that the gypsies can dance freely. Free the libraries and the universities; restore my dignity. Restore Iraq so it may bloom in vivid color. Let the world see the beauty of Iraq—the beauty of a land that is vibrant and alive.

I awoke, realizing it was all a dream. In reality, thieves landed between two rivers and stole the innocence and dignity of Iraq over and over again. They left us with nothing to be proud of and nothing to teach our children. Who will sing in Iraq? Who will paint great works? Who will dance, learn, drink, and thrive? Everything is lost within a great shadow. Iraq is dead.

During my sixteen years in America, nightmares still plague my sleepless nights. I sit awake searching for answers. I turn to my television; there are never answers there. I feel my chest; my heart still beats. I realize I am alive. I am alive in California.

In Iraq, every morning was a celebration. If you awoke at all, it was something to celebrate. Since I was born in 1959, I have had 11,215 celebrations in Iraq. In Iraq, I still have brothers, relatives, friends, memories, a history, and lovers. How do they all feel? Do they feel free or imprisoned? Do they celebrate now, even though they are at war? How can I sing if they are weeping?

I will take my mother's advice: any day you feel happy, that is a day to celebrate. That is your birthday, your anniversary, your Christmas and Easter, your vacation, your weekends and holidays.

Art of Paul Batou "Beauty of Mesopotamia"

Art of Paul Batou "Old houses in Baghdad-shanashil"

Memories

Do you remember Al Salihia and the Kremat?
Al Bataween and Al Shuhadah?
Al Rasafah and Al Karkh?
Midan Square?
Al Aathamia?
Suk Al Thahab?
Al Shurga,
And Abu Nuwas?

Iraqi Prayers

I cry, "Oh, God!" when I am poor.
I cry, "Oh, God!" when I am hungry.
I cry, "Oh, God!" when I am tired.
And I cry out, "Oh, God!" when I receive a bullet.

Confession

Do you know that my soul is full of sins?
I stopped in the rain,
To wash,
I cried.

The rain soaked my body,
And left streaks on my face;
It did not purify my soul.

I went to church,
I came to my knees,
And offered my prayers;
I took communion,
It did not purify my soul.

The statue of the virgin was painted,
With my best colors,
I pleaded, burdened by my sins.

Do you know that my sin is Iraq?
My sins are Babylon and Sumer.
Why did we hold the sons of God captive from Jerusalem?
And carried the curse of Torah and the Gospel!
Why did we follow Islam's banner?
And the great occupation?

Did you know,
They had instructed
Our ancestors on how to wield weapons?
And how to kill their neighbors?
They opened doors of exile.

Do you know that the rain,
Draws my tears like streams?
And makes me cry rivers?
Each drop hits my body,
As a cold bullet,
That does not hurt or kill me,
But just scars my soul.

My soul is burdened by sin.
We were told that confession washes away our sins.
I confessed to stealing a dinar,
I confessed I lied.
I will speak the truth,
To wash this sin away.
But how do I confess about Iraq's sins?
How do I reverse the history of Iraq,
If it is God's will?

Dreams

Once I dreamed of narrow alleys,
On Kremat's shanashil.

I dreamed of children with eyes,
And women with hearts.

I dreamed of the confused young,
And mothers on the streets of Baghdad;
Searching for bread and oil,
And for a cup of tea.

I wondered: why am I here?
While they are starving there?

My friend!
In Baghdad, my memories were
Sketched in shades of pain.
I forsake my friends for a glass of wine,
I etched my sadness on a layer of ceramic.

Who is going to play the guitar?
Who is going to declaim the words of Badr?
Who is going to sing . . . for the wine?

Where am I?
Far from the northern air,
Far from the southern scent,
From the noise of the city,
And the dawn prayer calling:
"God is great!"
Where am I?
Like a migrating bird,
That will return home.

Once I dreamed:
I was on Saddon Street,
Stopped at Victory Plaza.
Why do they call it Victory Plaza?
We never won any war.
I walked south,
To the eastern gate,
I saw Jawad and a horse.

I dreamed:
I was near the martyr monument,
I heard voices, all cursing the war.
I got up, just to end the sound of bullets and weeping.

I dreamed:
I was near Victory Arc,
A knight on a white horse,
Holding Iraq's flag,
Among soldiers and militia.
We won in Baghdad,
We lost much more than that.

I kept dreaming,
With open eyes,
In Uncle Sam's state.

Baghdad

Baghdad!
When will my body reach you?
I am waiting . . .
Behind closed windows!
I am cursing fate,
My birth . . .
I am cursing the roads,
And its poor and miserable people.

Bars of the dead,
White horses . . .
When will I finally reach you?
Old houses . . .
Old houses that lean on
My chest and my shoulders.

Why are women weeping?
Why are the poor crying?
Why are prostitutes, the homeless,
Drunks, and lovers screaming?

Baghdad!
I will not wash away your sins,
I am not the messiah.

The flooding ocean has overtaken me.
My dreams scattered in countries,
And countries.
Murderers and crows tear my body.
I was left afloat,
On the flooding ocean.

From Mesopotamia

Once you were Sumerian,
Or from Uruk.
Your wide eyes burned away my paper.
Where should I sketch my poetry?
On my chest? Or maybe on rocks?

I engraved my childhood in Kremat,
I hid between the alleys,
I looked into the eyes of women;
My heart was young,
And fresh, like an orange.
I don't know if I had ever loved you . . .
Or any of the others!

I saw you a thousand times,
I saw you yesterday, and a long while ago.
I saw you take nothing, and steal everything!

Once you were Sumerian,
In an era that knew no history.
You were Babylonian,
In a period that knew no love!

Walls hid our saga,
Nights had overheard what had happened!

You, daughter of Mesopotamia;
What dream are you awaiting?
Badr had passed away,
Yet, the rain is still pouring.
Sumer, Babylon, and Uruk have fallen,
And still, you are the daughter of them all!

Behind your fence,
There was a war,
Terror, and a tornado,
Dark sadness,
And vultures
Hovering the dead.

Come . . . touch me, part by part.
Come . . . touch my decayed bones.

In Love with Ishtar

Ishtar, where am I?
Facing toward the black eyes.
Was my name carved on rocks from Uruk?
Was an obelisk built?
Was a hanging garden constructed?

Did my lips leave the myth of love upon you?
Did they leave a trace?
A thousand years ago,
Did I know of Tammuz, or the March rains?
Did I build Ur's stairway?
Did you forget
That I am just human,
And not a God?

Ishtar,
If you had been the rushing river.
You could have washed away my filth!
Why were you not the raging inferno?
You could have burned away the winter from my soul!
Why were you not the rain,
Which flowed across my cheek, instead of these tears?

Ishtar,
My soul can no longer withstand summer or winter,
Day or night,
Weeping or joy,
A breeze or a storm.
You are my lover, my goddess!

Come, and have me!
Love me a thousand times!
Come, face me,
Lock your eyes onto mine,
Restore my body!

Bit by bit,
Piece by piece,
On roofs,
In alleys,
In airports,
Along beaches,
And on mountains.
Come,
Be my haven
In which I can anchor myself
In the worst of floods.

I am in a home unlike Babylonian homes.
I am in an alley unlike Babylonian alleys.
They had put my coffin in a grave,
Unlike Babylonian graves.
I have learned a language,
Unlike the language of Babylon.
I have loved a woman, and women,
They are unlike you, you who are of Babylon!

Come, and save me
From one God,
From one Allah
From one religion.
Come, we will return together,
To pray at Enlil's temple,
Below the glowing light of Shamash!
Take me back to Uruk's goddess!
For there,
in my own country,
They are allowed to spill my blood.

Ishtar, your soothing eyes are my harbor,
My passport to my haven;
They are the windows of my prison.

Ishtar, come, save me!
In Iraq, I was never free,
And my freedom, in exile,
I cannot enjoy.

Identity

I am not Assyrian or Chaldean or Akkadian.
I am not a Christian or Muslim or Buddhist.
I am human.
I was born in Mesopotamia, Uruk, Nippur, Shuruppak, and Sippar.
I was born in Babylon, home of Anu and Ishtar.
I am a son of Enlil, Shamash, and Gilgamesh.
I am a son of Ishtar, Ea, and Nunsun.
I was killed once by a flood,
And a million times by a creature,
Called human,
Called a country.
I was killed by a nation,
Or United Nations.

War and Cross

Wind blows . . .
Palm tree branches sway south.
Wind blows . . .
Palm tree branches sway north.
Rain falls
Tigris and Euphrates quench thirst
And orange trees in Balad . . .
Hide between the swaying palms
Seeking warmth.

Oh, Baghdad!
Are there still fishermen in Kremat?
Are there drunks in Abu Nuwas?
Did Jawad stay in downtown square?
And in Fardous, is there a rock or a statue?

Oh, Iraq . . . Iraq!
How much more blood is needed to quench your thirst?
Thieves join . . .
To kill lambs and humans!
And nations are watching,
A dying church and a dying mosque!

I carried a cross
In Herta
In Ur and Karbala.
I paid no taxes
Nor did I fight them.
My blood was spilled on Basra's soil.
My blood was in Kuwait, and in Najaf.
My blood was in Baghdad, and in Tikrit.
In Mousel, and all northern villages.

Thieves carried the cross,
They came to help.
They killed a nation and nations.
They will leave.
They will burn the remains of my body.
And generations will remember . . .
Babylon and Uruk.
They will remember Ashur and Ishtar,
And once in Sippar
We played the harp for
Fool nations.

My Village

I am from a tiny village to the north,
We had a rooster crow every morning,
There were so many trees,
With branches that were home to many birds.
We had a horse, cows, and sheep,
Neighbors, relatives, and my mother.
We had much wood to kindle,
And fires all the time.
Spring water moved into the fields and farms,
Like arteries and veins,
Breathing new life to all the walnut and fig trees.
We had grapevines that shadowed the hills,
We had mountains.
We heard dogs bark,
Children were at play,
Men tilling and sowing the fields,
The elderly relaxing behind the walls,
In the shade,
Whispering to each other.
We had a church,
Built by seven men.
Buried over seven men.
It was one night,
When savages and Kurds,
Moved across the wood,
From the mountains,
Over the roofs.
They destroyed walls,
Crucified my dreams,
Spilled our blood into the spring water.
We escaped,
And God looked away,
Away from my aunt, father, brothers, and neighbors.

Journey with Ishtar

Too many years have passed,
It seems that life is one long marathon.
We are not looking behind,
Or to the left or right,
Just forward.
In all Arab countries, there are plazas,
Or statues,
Dedicated to victory.
In all Arab countries, there you are;
My brothers, sisters, father, friends, and relatives.
In all Arab countries, they have bars,
Belly dancers, and lovers with broken hearts.
All Arab countries have a word
For "God is the greatest" or "Thank you, God."
In all Arab countries there are poems,
Pencils, papers,
And a butcher knife.
I am here,
And you are across an entire ocean.
Between us is a body of water,
Between us is a land called Iraq,
Between us is Baghdad, Sumer, Uruk, Babylon,
And a tiny village to the north,
Between us is a silence.
I am here now,
In the land of fog and blue eyes.
I left my history behind,
I lived on many streets,
And traveled into many stations.
I was afraid to be left behind,
And not rewarded like Gilgamesh.

I cut out pictures of memories,
And planted a flower on the forehead of every beauty,
It was like a thousand and one Arabian nights.
My dream is to be taken away by a gypsy caravan,
To the other side,
Where I can clean my face from sadness and tears.
My dream is to relocate for one hour,
In a bar in downtown Baghdad.
Listen to the folk songs from Youssif Omar,
See the sorrow in Iraq.
We have been told that we won the war in Baghdad,
But we lost our history, humanity, and dignity.
Ishtar,
I am here,
And you are on the other side.
Let me dream,
Let me wish,
Let me cry with no tears,
My body is weak,
And my face is still.
Just like a nightmare,
When strangers and thieves broke into my home,
And stole my memories and my history,
There was no sky and no moonlight,
Only smoke and darkness,
For they are evil.
Ishtar,
Iraq is dead.
Let me sleep, drink, and forget,
Take me to the other side of the ocean,
Where everyone is poor, homeless, and waiting for my arrival.
I need only bread, water,
Rice, and some clay from Sumer.
I can sleep in a small alley,
In Kremat.
There I will drink bitter tea,
It will be a long time before I taste anything sweet.
Take me to the other side,

Where a belly dancer dances.
I will see her face,
Her hair,
Her eyes,
I will watch her swing left and right.
She doesn't realize we are both from a land called Iraq,
We both speak Arabic,
And we both have broken hearts.
Ishtar,
Tonight a gypsy will sing for me alone,
Listen and imagine,
My sorrow and name in every word and sentence.
Tonight a gypsy will dance.
You can see,
How my soul will die on the floor.
My concern,
Everyone will know my name,
Will know that I am from Uruk.
My dear,
I cannot give love.
When my hand trembles, I cannot hold a brush,
Or pick a guitar,
Or listen to Neruda poems,
Or see Goya paintings.
I will die in love,
Waiting for a gypsy caravan to take me away.
Ishtar,
You left me in Iraq,
Like a broken chair in an empty room,
With a picture hanging on a dirty wall.
I became empty as a shelf in the Baghdad Library,
In a museum that only has a picture of my father.
Take me to my village,
Where I can clean my face in pure water,

Where I will sing with birds,
A song for sadness and a dream that never ends.
Ishtar,
A thousand girls will take my broken heart,
Will wipe my tears and sorrow.
Please,
Take me to a café,
Where people sleep,
And dance,
Without love or dreams.
Ishtar,
We never paid taxes,
We never engaged in war,
Yet we surrendered to Islam.
Take me to the other side of the ocean,
For I can cry with tears for only one cause.
Between us is a sky,
And an ocean.
We live as strangers in different lands.
We live as drunks with no alcohol.
Do you know that in Iraq,
There were bars and prostitutes too?
They speak Arabic, Assyrian, and Kurdish.
They speak the languages of Iraq,
But they don't have the sadness that we do.
They have been dead for a long time,
They insulted God and the earth,
For we carry the world's sins.
Oh, Ishtar,
Leave me alone.
I am awakened,
I am alive,
My eyes are open,
In a land called America.

Iraqi Freedom

Between the Tigris and the Euphrates,
I left my sorrow; I left my history, placed in a hall
Or museum, a place that describes my legends, and my father's tales,
We were Assyrian, Chaldean, Babylonian or Akkadian.
Our story ends with a cry from a woman,
In a land called Iraq, in a town named Baghdad.
My sadness is written on rocks and clay,
Placed in museums around the planet.
My stories and sadness were stolen by strangers and thieves.
In Jaikour, they cry Oh Badr!
In Uruk there is another cry Oh Badr!
Ali? What are the reasons for your tears?
Your arms? Or your burned body?
Your legs?
Baghdad?
Al Tahrir Plaza?
Jawad?
Gilgamesh?
Enlil?
Baghdad Library?
Al Saddon Street? Or Iraq's palm trees?
Your pain, the pain of all mothers, the elderly,
They left us nothing to be proud of or to die for.
Where are you, God? Why do you punish the people who love you?
Or are you like a nation's leader? Kills the poor and makes them suffer.
To whom shall I complain to?
Where are you, God? Who will listen to my pain?

Iraqi Marriage

Awaken, bride, awaken!
Today is your wedding day.
We will display flowers,
Roses of red and yellow in every balcony.
For life is like a wheel,
It rolls and rolls,
Fill glasses with wine,
Let us drink,
Let the music be loud, the bride wants to dance,
She is pretty, more than gold,
And her breasts are like a rock from Uruk.
She is tall, like a Basra palm tree.
Bring the wine and fill the glasses,
Let us drink and drink,
With every drink, an Iraqi will die.
Women are everywhere, girls on the streets,
Boys playing the drums,
And the sunlight fills every dark corner in the house,
The elderly peering through the windows,
Awaken, bride, awaken!
Today is a wedding day,
All the beautiful girls desire a kiss,
Kids want to play,
Bring the wine; there are plenty of grapes,
Let us drink and drink,
With every drink, an Iraqi will die.

Village Called Tin

Did you know,
The people in my village do not know how to write their names.
How about their legends,
Or tales,
Their history or songs.
They are farmers,
In a tiny village called Tin,
Embraced by a valley called Supna.
They have no border,
They have only names.
And the blue sky will capture their dreams,
While the green fields cover their secrets.
They are people of God,
They are simple,
They are honest,
They are pure.
They pray and fast,
They have patience and passion.
Their dreams and secrets were hidden,
In a vinery,
Between tobacco leaves,
And under walnut trees.
Their tears, sweat, and blood flew with
Spring water,
Across the fields between canyons,
And Swartuka mountain became green.
Under the church they buried seven deaths,
Under the church they buried seven dreams,
Under the church they buried seven secrets.
It was a sound of bullets,
It was a sound of horses,
And light from fires.
A silence broken

By the cry of a child.
They shout "run!"
"Run!"
"Run into a city called Baghdad!"
Oh Baghdad!
Your rooms are small,
Your alleys are narrow.
Where to hide?
Baghdad . . . Oh, Baghdad!
You are a whore with endless stories.
You are a whore with no dreams,
And with no lovers,
Baghdad,
You have become ugly like a devil,
You have become dirty like garbage.
Nations, invaders, thieves, looters,
And liars.
They left your body with bloody wounds,
And scars.
Baghdad, tell me how will your broken body
Hold our cries and hunger?
How will your ruined beauty nurture our dreams and secrets?
They shout again and again,
Run into the countries!
Lay down in stations and airports.
Over the seas and across the oceans.
Between lovers and strangers,
With no identity,
With no dreams.
Smile,
You are in America,
Look over the sky,
There is a very tiny star,
That shines over Tin too.
Smile for the birds that fly over Tin.
Smile when the flowers bloom color over Tin.
Smile when the dreams and secrets remain,
In a tiny village called Tin.
Smile, you are in America,
But born in Iraq.

Army Camp

Rain falls,
On tinplate roofs.
It sounds like cold bullets.

On the nearby hills,
Water flows as a river!
Tell me!
Why do I fear,
The sound of rain?

Wet under drops of rain.
Tell me!
Why do I fear
While looking behind windows,
Hearing children and women wailing,
Lovers' moans,
Prostitutes and drunks?

How can I calm down?
Guards are shouting,
And the cold covers my fingers.
How can I silence
The women looking at my snowy face?
Tell me!
How can I dream while standing?
How can I die,
When I have been dead,
For more than two thousand years?

Minor Dreams

I am a kid,
Born in Iraq.
My dreams were minor,
A cup of milk or water to drink,
A crayon to color,
A pencil to write,
A book to read,
A toy to play with,
A friend to talk to,
A pet to love,
A father to listen to,
A mother to hug,
A bed to sleep,
A home to rest,
A light to see with,
A school to study at,
A song to listen to,
A country to grow in.
I am a kid,
Born in Iraq,
My dreams were sanctioned,
Shame on you all.

To a Friend

I know,
You are from Iraq,
You speak the language of Iraq,
You hold the name of Iraq,
So am I.

Distances are between us.
We live in countries that teach us
Estrangement.
We live like drunks without alcohol,
Or drugs.
Do you know?
That in Iraq,
There are bars,
And prostitutes.
They speak the language of Iraq,
But they do not suffer as we do;
We carry Iraq's sins.
You do not know,
How eagles flew over Baghdad,
How the storms and desert sand blew into alleys and through houses.
Women wailing, children screaming,
Break the calmness of the silence.
It was dark, and an ocean of starving and crushing flows.
Oh dear, we are unable to resist as walls do.

Invasion

More than two thousand years ago,
We lost Mesopotamia,
We lost the Babylonian walls,
The Hanging Gardens were destroyed,
Ea and Ishtar left,
Gilgamesh finally died.
Between the two rivers the strangers landed,
They spoke a language of God,
They spoke the language of jihad.
They killed for rewards,
Of virgins in the sky.
A strange God,
Not like you, Shamash.
A strange God,
Not like you, Enlil.
I was asked,
To give up my beliefs,
To give up my freedom,
To give up my life,
To give up my language,
To give up my soul,
Under the judgment of swords.
More than two thousand years ago,
The name of God woke me,
With a bloom of dawn,
And the sunset over the Tigris River.
Oh, Baghdad, my body is barren,
Who will fill it with soul?
Oh, Baghdad, my cheeks are barren,
Who will fill them with happiness?
Oh, Baghdad, my eyes have dried,
Who will fill them with tears?

Baghdad Morning in New York

At eyeshot,
Such threads of gloomy fog
in a coal black sky.
They claim to be God's knights
And universe's earthquake
They claim to be . . . the message's protector

At eyeshot.
A blast echoes . . .
Holes scorched in the sky.

At eyeshot,
There was silence.
And waiting.

Towers fell down from the clouds,
The ground collected
The scattered bodies.
There was . . . a storm of crying.
And screaming.
All were hugging the air.

Drizzles of smoke drop,
Fall like a rain shower
Over the heaps.
I looked at my face in the mirror!

When evening came along,
City lights shined
On remains and corpses.
Is this another Baghdad?
One that collects its dead!
And sings a song at the Euphrates.

Blue was the sky,
Silent was the ocean.
While embracing the city,
And the Statue of Liberty.
Oh . . . New York.

Do they come from there?
Chasing us?
Let them come,
My heart is full of snow,
from winter and wintertime.
My heart is full of anger,
from fighting and killing.
My heart is full of sadness,
from weeping and mourning.
A wound has opened,
A tower has fallen!

My dear,
They do not love flowers,
Or jasmine.
They do not like farmers' songs,
Nor do they like the rain.
They do not like fall whistling,
Or the summer sun rising.
They do not like winter nights.

At eyeshot,
Wherever I look,
I saw light.
I saw old people and children.
I saw orphans and heroes.
All are lifting
A tower
To the sky.
Oh . . . New York.
Oh . . . Baghdad.
Cowards are they,
Who kill from behind.

Graveyard

Gilgamesh!
Do not weep.
Enkidu died.
Worms devoured his beauty.
Leave him in peace.
In Anu's temple,
He killed Humbaba.
He killed the devil.
In order for people to live in peace!
Ishtar!
Do not weep.
Gilgamesh died.
A snake ate his plant.
Leave him in peace.
In your temple,
He killed Humbaba.
He killed the devil.
In order for people to live in peace!
Enlil!
Do not weep.
Mesopotamia died.
Killed by Humababa.
Killed by devils.
Killed by nations.
Killed by people.
Anu!
Do not weep.
The Land of Uruk has become a graveyard.
The Hanging Gardens has become a graveyard.
All of Babylon has become a graveyard.
Even Nineveh has become a graveyard.
Ea!
Do not weep.
All of Iraq has become a graveyard.

God and I

When the dawn began to glow,
I raised my head up
And cried out to god
"Why . . . God?"
Babylon was cursed.
When the dawn began to glow,
I looked into the sky.
My lips are buzzing,
My hands are shaking,
My face is still,
And my body is falling apart.
God, your judgment is unfair.
Your punishment is harsh.
We are your children.
We built long gates around Babylon.
We had warriors, legendary animals,
And stones to guard.
When the darkness shadowed the earth,
I raised my head into the sky,
And cried out to God:
"Why are we cursed?"
My sadness is deep within me.

Traveling over a long distance,
Crossing the ocean,
Among strangers,
Women everywhere,
People are laughing,
Birds are flying,
Life is moving,
Lights are shining,
Buildings are high,
Yet, I hide my face like a bride.
My sadness is deep,
With a smile on my face.
Listen people!
I have no fear.
I am not from Iraq,
I am not from Mesopotamia.
I am not Babylonian,
Nor Akkadian
I am not an Arab . . . nor American:
I am just human.

Nightmare

I closed my eyes
In a new land: America.
The sound of jazz music,
The sound of birds outside in the garden,
The sound of a language, it is not Arabic.
It is not Baghdad,
It is not Mesopotamia,
Nor Sippar.
It is not the sound of Babylon's harp,
Or the mosque of Allah Akbar.
Oh, long nights,
Between your dark layers
My lips are silent,
My eyes are closed.
Still, there is a war back there.
Still my name shadows the history of a wounded land.
Tomorrow will be a new day,
I will start a new life.
As in Iraq,
Every day I awake in Baghdad.
It is my birthday.
I have lived for 11,215 days,
Choose one to celebrate.
Tomorrow I will write a poem.
I will dance.
I will sing.
I will play my guitar.

Anyone in America will listen.
Anyone will listen to a long scary story.
A story began with Shamash, Gilgamesh, Enkidu, and Tammuz.
A story ended with one rule and one order.
A story ended with humiliation and torture of my soul.
Jawad, your statue of freedom is still in Baghdad.
Badr, your graveyard is still in Jaikour.
I am far, far from Tin.
I am in America.
I opened my eye after a nightmare.
I touch my body piece by piece.
I touch my bones.
My eyes, my toes.
My hand is shaking.
I closed my eyes again,
Open them slowly,
Jump out to the street,
Open my windows,
Turn on the TV,
Turn on the radio;
Do I hear any Arabic words?
No.
I touch my body again.
I am alive.
I am not in Iraq;
I am in America.

Iraqi Love

Baghdad, I loved you
When I had no desire for love.
Will your Sumerian eyes
Shadow my sadness and pain.
Baghdad, I loved you
When I had no desire for life.
Your wide eyes along the sunset,
See my dreams.
Baghdad . . . Oh, Baghdad!
When will my body and soul reach you?
Baghdad, I loved you
When I had no desire to die.
My face is looking
Through closed windows.
My lips are crucified,
And my voice is silent.
I accept my destiny.
Waiting for a long time,
Waiting and waiting more than a hundred years
I was dead once and many times.
I am too tired to love,
And feel sorrow.
Let me cry facing you.
Let me cry facing shanashil.
Baghdad, I loved you.
When I had no desire for love.
I saw you far away,
I saw you very close,
I see you when I am asleep,
I see you when I am awake,
Yet I can not speak
My lips are crucified,
And my body is ravaged by thieves.
My soul is flying
In your empty allies

My soul is crying for dreams,
Baghdad,
When will our story end?
Please, tell me.
I can no longer listen to
Women wailing,
Poor . . . hopeless . . . homeless . . . men's shouting
I can no longer listen to
Children crying.
Baghdad, I loved you.
When I had no desire for love.
Along Tigris,
Along the river,
The fish smell,
The dead smell,
The water smells.
The soil becomes red.
Baghdad
When will our story end?
I can no longer
Drink bitter coffee
Mixed with Iraqi blood.
Blood that has a name . . . address . . . love.
Has a mother and friends.
Has a soul . . . had a dream.
Baghdad,
I need to write your abandoned name
On people's faces.
Your name will become the address of neighbors and strangers.
Baghdad, I loved you.
When I had no desire for love.
How can I drip my blood
In your cold hands?
How will I plant a jasmine flower
On your forehead?
How can I feel proud
Holding your memory in my heart?
How can I mention your name
When my lips are crucified?
And my body is tortured by strangers.
Baghdad,

I am like a lover who waited too long
On a harbor
For a ship that never came.
I am like a dead man who dies again and again
Baghdad, I loved you
When I had no desire for love.
will your wide eyes like a Sumerian queen
Hide my sorrow,
Hide my sadness,
Hide my childhood stories,
Hide my colors,
Hide my words and my poems,
Hide my soul and my love.
Baghdad, I loved you
When I had no desire for love.
When I can reach you
Facing you,
Looking into your eyes,
I have been waiting for a long, long time.
I am tired.
I am older now by a thousand years.
Baghdad,
On your street curbs, I ripped my photos,
My memories,
My stories from wall to wall,
My love.
My lips are crucified,
My voice is silent,
Baghdad, I loved you
When I had no desire for love.
Do not hide from Shamash,
Or Enlil.
Ishtar
Will restore your beauty.
We can build Uruk again.
Do not hide
From Gilgamesh;
He will rewrite your legends.
We can build Babylon again.
We will sing in Sippar.
We can rebuild the Ashur library.

We can play the harp again
For the earth,
For the poor,
For our sadness,
For our dreams,
For our children.
To thrive in peace again.
Baghdad, I loved you
When I had no desire for love.
Between your wide eyes
Like a Babylonian queen
I will sleep for one final night,
I will dream for one final night,
I will die again for the last time.
I will cry.
Can your cold hands
Hold my tears?
Can your eyes
Reach my naked body?
Baghdad,
My lips are crucified,
My voice is silent.
Baghdad,
You became my love,
My birthplace,
My sorrow.
You became a book with blank pages
To write my poems in,
To write my story in.
You became a canvas.
A wall to draw my pictures on,
Or to throw my colors on.
You became the candle
To lift this darkness.
Baghdad, I loved you
When I had no desire for love.
When can I see you again?
To say
Good-bye again.

Conclusion

Iraq is not the only place with oppression; the oppressed are everywhere. In every country, across every land, the oppressed reside. Suffering is a universal trait. Who can withstand the travesties of war or epidemic diseases? Who can rise against the never-ending hunger that ravages so many lands or the murder of entire races?

Wealthy countries provide weapons and humanitarian aid at the same time to underdeveloped countries. The only real solution is to drop our weapons and come together in peace. Education is the key to this dream.

People need music, fine art, and articulate poetry. People need nature and fresh air more than they need money. Many years ago, I considered why UNICEF could not deliver a better education to the world. Why could they not unify the education around the world and bring the same books to classrooms everywhere so that American or German children read the same texts as children in Africa, Afghanistan, or Iraq? In an ideal world, all children in all places would have the best possible education. Maybe future generations will consider that a good education is the foundation of a better world.

If I were asked what I would tell every parent in the world, I would respond with the urgency of parents to send their children to school and be more involved in their progression. Teach your children to love music and art, to appreciate great works. These words are from an Iraqi artist who, through turmoil and oppression, became a pharmacist, painter, and writer. These words are from an Iraqi, who wants to pass the same dream on to the world.

Glossary

This glossary lists places, people, and events mentioned in this book.

Abu Nuwas—A riverside along Tigris in downtown Baghdad. Named after Abu Nuwas, a poet from the Abbasid period AD 749-1180.

Akkadian—One from the empire named after the city of Akkad ca. 2350 BC.

Al Aathamia—City in Baghdad.

Al Rasafah—Baghdad divided by the Tigris River into two regions, one of them is Al Rasafah; the other is Karkh.

Al Salihia and Kremat—Cities in Baghdad where I spent my childhood after migrating from my village in northern Iraq.

Al Shuhadah—Plaza in Baghdad, *shuhada* means "martyrs" in English.

Al Shurga—Major marketplace in Baghdad.

Al Tahrir Plaza—Square in downtown Baghdad, *tahrir* means "liberate."

Anu—Sky god in Sumeria.

Ali—Iraqi child who lost his family, legs, and hand. His body was burned during the "Iraqi Freedom" war.

Allah—"God" in English.

Allah Akbar—Meaning "God is the greatest" in Arabic.

Ashur—religious capital of Assyria

Assyrian—One from the empire of Assyria ca. 1600 BC.

Babylon—Ancient city founded after the collapse of Ur in 2004 BC.

Badr—Famous Iraqi poet born in Jaikour. He mentioned Jesus Christ in many of his poems, even though he was a Muslim.

Balad—City in northern Baghdad known for palm and orange trees.

Basra or Basrah—Major city in the southern border toward Kuwait.

Bataween—City occupied mostly by Christians near downtown Baghdad.

Chaldean—One from the Chaldean Empire ca. 626 BC.

Dinar—Currency in Iraq.

Ea—The god of the subterranean freshwater sea.

Enlil—Sumerian word meaning "God."

Fardous Square—A famous plaza in downtown Baghdad.

Gilgamesh—King who ruled the city of Uruk ca. 2700 BC.

Herta—Chaldean ancient town in southern Iraq.

Humbaba—monstrous guardian of the forest of cedar.

Ishtar—The goddess of love and war.

Jawad—A famous painter and sculptor. His statue of freedom is in downtown Baghdad.

Jaikour—village where Iraqi poet badr was born

Karbala—Holy city for Shiite Muslims in southern Iraq.

Mesopotamia—The area between the Euphrates and Tigris rivers now called Iraq.

Midan—Square in Baghdad where the Ministry of Defense is located.

Mosque—Holy place for Muslims to pray.

Mousel—City in northern Iraq. Also called Nineveh, an ancient city from the Assyrian Empire.

Najaf—Holy city for Shiite Muslims in southern Iraq.

Nineveh—an ancient city from the Assryian Empire, now called Mousel.

Nippur—The religious capital of Enlil located in the center of Mesopotamia.

Nunsun—The divine mother of Gilgamesh.

Saddon Street—Main street in downtown Baghdad with shops, hotels, restaurants, etc.

Shamash—The sun god who opposed evil.

Shanashil—Traditional design of windows made of wood and painted with different colors. They are located in the upper level of the building.

Shuruppak—Ancient city of Sumer, located in northern Uruk.

Sippar—City of sun god in northern Babylon.

Suk Al Thahab—Jewelry marked in Baghdad. The word *thahab* means "gold."

Sumer—One from the Sumerian civilization ca. 3000.

Tammuz—God of nature, he is the lover and husband of Ishtar.

Tikrit—City in northern Baghdad. Birthplace of Saddam.

Tin—Tiny village in northern Iraq near the border of Turkey. It was my birthplace. It is known for the collapse of its church during roof construction; seven people died. The village was later destroyed by Kurds.

Uruk—Ancient city of Sumeria.

Victory Plaza—Located on Saddon Street in downtown Baghdad.

Youssif Omar—A folksinger.

Index

N

Najaf, 44
Nineveh, 60
Nippur, 42
Nunsun, 42

P

poetry
  "Army Camp", 54
  "Baghdad", 37
  "Baghdad Morning in New York", 58
  "Confession", 33
  "Dreams", 35
  "From Mesopotamia", 38
  "God and I", 61
  "Graveyard", 60
  "Identity", 42
  "In Love with Ishtar", 40
  "Invasion", 57
  "Iraqi Freedom", 50
  "Iraqi Love", 65
  "Iraqi Marriage", 51
  "Iraqi Prayer", 32
  "Journey with Ishtar", 46
  "Memories", 31
  "Minor Dreams", 55
  "My Village", 45
  "Nightmare", 63
  "To a Friend", 56
  "Village Called Tin", 52
  "War and Cross", 43
poor, 37
prostitutes, 37

R

religion, 41

S

sadness, 24, 26, 35, 39, 47, 49, 50, 59, 61, 65, 68
sanctions, 25
Shamash, 41, 42, 57, 64, 67
shanashil, 21, 35, 65
Shuruppak, 42
sin, 22, 33
Sippar, 42, 44, 63, 67
sky, 58
soldiers, 24
Statue of Liberty, 59
Suk Al Thahab, 31
Sumer, 15, 23, 26, 33, 38, 39, 46, 47, 65
Supna, 52

T

Tammuz, 40, 64
Tigris, 22
Tikrit, 44
Tin, 21, 64

U

UNICEF, 69
United Nations, 42
Uruk, 23, 38, 40, 41, 42, 44, 46, 50, 51, 60, 67

V

Victory Plaza, 36

W

women, 37

Y

Youssif Omar, 47